Lord,
I am so prone to
Extravagant extremes:
I either foolishly
Justify my imperfections
Or I frantically bemoan them.
All the while You wait for me
To release them — to You.

LORD, YOU LOVE TO SAY YES is a spiritual
accounting of life's deficits and liabilities,
and a joyous summing up of all that is
best . . . something we may have forgotten.

Lord, You Love to Say Yes

Ruth Harms Calkin
Illustrated by Kinuko Craft

David C. Cook Publishing Co.
ELGIN, ILLINOIS—WESTON, ONTARIO

David C. Cook Publishing Co., Elgin IL 60120

Printed in the United States of America
Library of Congress Catalog Number: 75-18923
ISBN: 0-912692-81-2

CONTENTS

5

YES!

Oh, dear God!
I've made a profound
And glorious discovery:
When the painful circumstances
Of my listless life
Shout a fanatic No
Jesus Christ, the Victorious One
Shouts an emphatic Yes.

CHAPTER ONE

Living Lessons

GIVE—LIVE

I cry to You, Lord,
But I find no help.

"Little one, *give* help."

I search for You, Lord,
But I see no way.

"Little one, *live* the Way."

ILLUSIVE DREAMS

Sometimes, Lord
I think I spend my entire life
Working toward illusive dreams.
I dream that someday things will be
Exactly as I want them:
I'll ride on the crest
Of my noble achievements.
With an easy-going independence
I'll keep my confident cool
My house will stay spotless
My budget will balance
My family will applaud me
My friends will acclaim me
I'll glow with charisma.
Lord, am I missing the mark?
Is there a chance for my dreams?

Child of My Plan
Seek first the Kingdom of God
And His righteousness
And every plan of Mine
Will exceed by far
All your illusive dreams.

PLAIN OLD ME

O Lord
Here I am again
Just plain old me
Coming to You
As I've come a thousand times—
And this is what always happens:
Your response is immediate
You open Your arms unhesitatingly
You draw me to Yourself
You clasp me to Your Father-heart.
Then You reaffirm my position:
I'm a child of the King
And all that is Yours is mine.
When I begin my stammering account
Of gross unworthiness
Your gentle smile hushes me.
With endless patience
You remind me once more
That my value never determines Your love.
Rather, Your love determines my value.

THE FACADE

Lord, I bow before You contritely
Confessing my shameful failures.
This whole wretched week
I've felt like a phony
And my actions have justified
My gnawing guilt.

Monday:
I spoke at a women's luncheon
And repeatedly emphasized
The joy of gentleness.
Then two hours later
I was angrily shouting at Jennifer.

Tuesday:
My widowed neighbor invited me in
For a cup of coffee.
I was simply "too busy."
Later that day I learned
Her beloved niece had been killed.

Wednesday:
"I'll pray as you have your checkup,"
I told my concerned friend.

Thursday:
My friend stopped by to thank me

For the prayer I neglected to pray.

Friday:
Over the phone I said sweetly:
"Don't give it a thought.
It's perfectly all right."
I was thinking—*how stupidly careless.*

Saturday:
I was tight with tension
Bone tired.
I was sure Aunt Sarah would call
So I didn't answer the phone.

Sunday:
Reverently sitting
In this quiet sanctuary
I wince to think of my subtle facade.
Purge me, Lord.
Shatter my pretense
Make me a glowing demonstration
Of the hymns I sing today
With such holy joy.

SPIRITUAL RETREAT

This was my calculated plan:
I would set aside my usual schedule—
The menial tasks that wedge in routinely.
In the peace and quiet of my living room
I would relax in Your glorious presence.
How joyfully I envisioned the hours—
My personal spiritual retreat!
With Bible and notebook beside me
I would study and meditate—
I would intercede for the needy world.

But how differently it happened, Lord:
Never has the phone rung so persistently.
Sudden emergencies kept pouring in
Like summer cloudbursts.
My husband came home ill.
There were appointments to cancel
Plans to rearrange.
The mailman brought two disturbing letters
A cousin whose name I couldn't remember

Stopped by on her way through town.
My morning elation became drooping deflation.

And yet, dear Lord
You were with me in it all!
I sensed Your vital presence—
Your sure and steady guidance.
Not once did You leave me stranded.
Perhaps, in Your great wisdom
You longed to teach me a practical truth:
When *You* are my Spiritual Retreat
I need not be a spiritual recluse.

Lord, I know I promised You
I'd accept Your plan for me
Willingly and gratefully—
But now I'm terribly confused.
How would I have responded
Had I *known* I'd be standing
In an endless production line
Cutting brown spots from fresh fruit?
Nothing else has worked out, Lord—
You know how I've tried.
Is this all You have in mind for me?
I feel so futile and stifled here—
So smothered with boredom.
There is no challenge
And the longings cut so deep.
Lord, I'm struggling to believe
There is no unfulfillment in You—
No purpose thwarted
So deliver me from my brooding
And enable me to accept with dignity
Your place and plan for me here.
You will guide me if there is more.
If not, help me to quietly adjust.
Today, Lord—*this very day*
Use me to lighten the burdens
Of those who work with me.
Above all, as I stand in line
May I produce the fruit of the Spirit.

How Else?

O Lord—
I am continually amazed
At Your willingness to work
Through my nothingness
And my simplicity.
I am always suggesting
That You wait
Until some future spring or fall
When I can offer You
A more polished, glittering self—
But the very things I struggle
To correct and improve
You want surrendered as they are.
You want to give Yourself
A magnificent reputation
By Your accomplishment in me.
So, dear Lord
Take my insignificance
And make it a shining emblem
Of Your creative power.
Do it all by Yourself.

Dear child, how else
Would it ever get done?

LORD, YOU LOVE TO SAY YES

Lord, I asked You for abundant life
Rich, challenging, full of adventure
And You said Yes.
I asked You for an undisturbable joy
Independent of transitory change
And You said Yes.
I asked You to thread my tears into a song
When I was shattered and torn with grief
And You said Yes.
I asked You to steady me when I staggered—
To hold me when I struggled
To seize me when I resisted
And You said Yes.
I asked You to forgive my vain grasping
My foolish fears, my willful pride
And You said Yes.
I asked You to be my Helper, my Friend
My Light in the darkness
And You said Yes.
I asked You to guide me all my life
With Your wisdom, Your counsel
Your captivating love
And You said Yes.
Sometimes, Lord
I feel like a spoiled child
Who gets whatever he asks for.
You overwhelm me with joy
For *You love to say Yes!*

THINK OF ME

For so many days
I've struggled with this hurt
The cutting words
The stinging resentment.
I *thought* she was my friend
I trusted her, upheld her
And now there is this stone wall
Of suspicion and distrust.
Oh, Lord
Such betrayal of friendship
Baffles and overwhelms me.
I'm haunted by the memory
Of her angry eyes
Her flaming face.
She left me gasping for breath—
So unfair was her accusation.
Yet—even now, dear Lord
The words I read so long ago
Come ringing like a distant bell:
"Let it be—think of Me."
Lord, empower me to do *this* day
What I know I must do ultimately
If Your love is my highest goal.

"Let it be—think of Me."

SACRILEGE

"That was great, my friend."
(Why wasn't I asked to do it?)

"Congratulations on your achievement."
(Why does he always succeed?)

"Your new home is charming."
(Some people have everything.)

Forgive me, God
For moments of sacrilege
When I have expressed good
While thinking evil.

HOSPITAL WARD

Forgive me, Lord—
I'm so irritable and restless
As I lie here uncomfortably
In this four-bed hospital ward.
I know I should express gratitude
To my nurse who is caring for me
With such professional efficiency.
But, Lord, I'm depressed today.
My body feels like a heavy weight
And I just don't want to be bothered.
I'm terribly ashamed to admit it
But I'm even repelled by cheerfulness.
I wish my nurse wouldn't smile so much
Or talk so fast or move so often.
My thoughts just can't keep up with her.
Lord, I cringe when she effervesces
With her subtle *we* and *our:*
"Now we'll take our temperature.
"Over on our left side now.
"Remember, we must wiggle our toes."

I wonder how she'd respond if I said:
"Must we really? Why don't *you* do it—
I'll just lie here and watch!"

Dear Lord, tell me—
I really want to know:
Is my negative attitude
A natural reaction to illness
Or am I revealing my true self?

FOOLISH COMPLAINTS

Lord, all day long
I've acted like a cranky old woman.
I've splattered complaints
In every room of our house:

I've complained about housework drudgery
About incessant interruptions
About bothersome necessities.
I've spouted off about our neighbor's dog
About the rising cost of food
About the incompetency of mail service.
I've let boredom and bitterness take root
And spring into a tree of self-pity
Shedding its sticky leaves
On every member of my family.

But now while I get ready for bed
My husband is listening
To his favorite newscaster.
In the background I hear:
"Fire destroys family of six."
"Frantic parents receive ransom note."

"Head-on collision paralyzes woman."
"Pakistan quake kills 7,000."
On and on it goes, dear Lord
And my foolish complaints are shamed.
Forgive my gross selfishness.
Enable me to accept eagerly
My personal responsibilities.
Lord, in some small way tomorrow
May I assuage the world's heartache
Without contributing to it.

SORRY, LORD

Lord—
That woman I had lunch with
Seems to be an authority
On every conceivable subject.
She quotes statistics
Faster than a secretary
Clicks typewriter keys.
There's no in-between for her:
She's vehemently for
Or vehemently against.
She knows where to shop
How to shop, when to shop.
She knows who's in and what's out.
Her vocabulary is stupendous.
(I wonder if she can spell the words?)
If you like ruffles and frills
She's beautifully groomed.
Her jewelry is authentic—
Anything but costume jewelry.
Just the same, Lord
I doubt that she can bake
An apple strudel like mine.

Dear child—
Is there something
You'd like to confess?

REMORSE

Today I shopped in a supermarket
Where shelves were crowded with food.
I made numerous choices.
I purchased every item on my list—
Even threw in a few delicacies.
Finally I stood at the checkstand
And to my deplorable shame
I echoed the familiar complaints
Of the woman standing next to me—
Her basket as loaded as mine.

And now the haunting memory
Wraps itself around my thoughts.
I think of the experts who tell us
There is no end in sight
To famine, drought, poverty, death.
Millions are plagued with starvation.
Yet, there I stood—a part of the horde
Spilling my indignant criticism.

Dear Lord, how I must grieve You.
Forgive me, I pray.
Alter my perspectives
And flood me with compassion.
Grip me with a firm determination
To reduce my standard of living
And increase my standard of giving.
Above all, dear Lord
Saturate my heart with gratitude.

LORD, IF YOU'LL JUST EXCUSE ME

Lord, I'll gladly write
A charity check for fifty dollars—
If You'll just excuse me
From loving that woman!
I'll entertain the minister
And sing in the choir—
I'll even teach a Bible class
If You'll just excuse me
From loving that woman!
Lord, I'm perfectly willing
To visit the sick
Write letters to shut-ins
Read to the blind—
If You'll just excuse me
From loving that woman!

It won't work, will it, Lord?
(I think I knew from the beginning.)
With all my benevolent offers
Your own Word keeps tripping me up:
"Beloved, if God so loved us

We ought also to love one another."
So, Lord, one of us must change.
As I see it, You've got
All the ingredients for a miracle.

"Dear child
My love flowing through you
Will change you both.
Just offer yourself as My channel."
"Is that all, Lord?"
"No. Then bake her an apple pie."
"Oh, dear Lord!"
"Don't fret, child;
A cherry pie will do just as well."

OUR PASTOR'S WIFE

Dear Lord—
Thank You for a vital and beautiful woman:
Our pastor's wife.
Thank You for her loyalty, her devotion
As she stands behind the man
Who stands behind the pulpit.
Thank You for her charm, her serenity
Her humility and patience.
Thank You for her deep compassion
Her listening heart
Her healing touch.
Thank You for her practical concern
And for her unshakable faith.

She carries no sham or pretense, Lord.
She wears no stilted mask.
She is as much at home in the balcony
With a row of collegians
As she is in the main sanctuary
With a silver-haired grandmother . . .
As much at home in the church kitchen
As she is at an elegant banquet . . .
As much at home at an annual retreat
As she is teaching a class of children.

Lord
In her genuine love we sense You.
In her radiant life we see You.
She is indeed Your chosen woman—
Our pastor's wife.

PHONE CALL

I answered the phone
And wished I hadn't.
Lord, she keeps talking and talking
And there's no way to stop her.
She asks a question
And gives her own answer.
In the middle of one story
She starts another.
Today she said lustily:
"Life is just rush rush rush."
I prayed that she'd rush
To her kitchen.

Lord, when she calls I feel trapped—
Pushed into a corner.
I want to say, "No, no
I haven't the time today."
Yet when I think of Your patience
I am gnawed by guilt.
Is it a false guilt, Lord?
I honestly think my emotions
Are more harmed
Than hers are helped.
Am I wrong?

Tell me, please tell me . . .
How would You handle such calls?

SPECIAL FRIENDSHIP

Lord, this morning I thank You
With renewed appreciation
For the exquisite gift of friendship
And for my special friend
With her happy heart
Whose life is so intertwined with mine.

Thank You for her healthy optimism
Her enduring values
Her child-like trust in You.
Thank You for her creativity
So expansively shared.
Thank You for her direct honesty
Her radiant enthusiasm
Her refreshing freedom.
Thank You for her listening ear
Her ready response to needs.
Thank You for the way
Our thoughts walk arm-in-arm.
Thank You that together
We can be utterly ourselves
Without pretense—
Without fear.
Thank You that we can pray together
Laugh and cry together
Cushion defeats
And applaud victories together.

Thank You most of all, dear Lord
That through the tested years
Our friendship proves to be
Another joyful way of knowing You.

STAY THERE

Lord
Please get me off
This emotional elevator
Which carries me so swiftly
From the basement of despair
To the tenth floor of exhilaration
And down to the basement again.
I'm hoarse from shouting
My fists are blue from pounding
I'm suffocating in this
Dark windowless box.

"Turn and look, dear child.
The door is wide open.
Walk straight into My waiting arms
And stay there."

MOMENT-BY-MOMENT

Lord, I thought I had
Given myself to You irrevocably.
I mean it, Lord.
I honestly thought
There would be no turning back
No secret side glances.
But now I shamefully hang my head:
I'm bewildered
I'm chagrined
By the frightening discovery
Of my unlimited capacity
For self-indulgence.
I'm beginning to understand
That my surrender must be
Moment-by-moment
As well as once-for-all.

FULFILLMENT

Lord, there's not a single thing
You couldn't accomplish without me.
Had I never been born
Your plan for the world
Would continue to unfold.
But You have graciously consented
To make my life a daily demonstration
Of Your magnificent power
In an earthen vessel—called me.

This indeed is fulfillment.

CHAPTER TWO

Learning His Love

REVERSAL

Lord
For so long
I thought Your love
Demanded that I change.
At last
I am beginning to understand
That Your love
Changes me.

ALL OPTIONS END

Thank You, Lord
For the sermon reminding me
That I don't take You
On the installment plan
With fingers crossed
Behind my back.
Nor do I take You on "approval"
To see how You'll work out.
You are the first word
And the last.
Nobody is going to tell me
What to do
I've already been told.
With You
All options end.

CELEBRATION

When I think of Your lavish goodness
The longings You've satisfied
The forgiveness You've granted
The promises You've kept
When I think of Your irresistible love
Your ceaseless care
Your unfailing protection . . .

O Lord God
I want to raise flags
And fly banners
And sound bugles.
I want to run with lighted torches
And praise You
From the mountaintop.
I want to write symphonies
And shout for joy.
I want to throw a festive party
For ten thousand guests.
I want to celebrate with streamers
And bright lights
And an elaborate banquet.

"Fine, dear child.
I'm ready."

DONKEY DAYS (I Samuel 9)

Dear God—
I just couldn't help it:
I chuckled aloud this morning
As I read the story of Saul—
How one very ordinary day
At the urgent request of his father
Saul combed the hillside
Searching for lost donkeys.
Little did he know
That Samuel waited to anoint him
That very day as Israel's first king.
The story refreshed and delighted me.
Far too often I bewail my daily routine.
My days with their nitty-gritty
Seem no more challenging
Than hunting for lost donkeys—
Stubborn obstinate donkeys.
But suddenly this morning
There came a flash of fresh insight:
You do indeed have a plan for me
You have a settled purpose
I am guided by Your wisdom and love
And all You ask is my confident trust.
Dreary days? Donkey days?
Yes, Lord—often.
But just around the corner
Or at the top of a hill
You wait with a shining surprise!

Your Word My Claim

O God—
With my total being
I have claimed Your promise
In my desperate need.
Your Word has become
So all-consuming
That it is written
As much in my heart
As in Your Book.
Now surely I can trust
The integrity of my Father.

LOVE RUSHING TOWARD ME

I stroll along the beach
Pressing my feet into warm sand.
I watch the crashing breakers
Come rushing toward the shore.
In each majestic wave
I catch a glimmer of Your love
Rushing toward me
Always toward me, God
And then I grasp anew
My urgent need
To stroll along the beach.

YOU ARE FREE

O God—
I read today
That the sons of Jacob
And their descendants
Had lived in Egypt 430 years.
But on the last day
Of the 430th year
Your people left Egypt
And the cruel bondage
They had painfully endured.
This was the time You selected.
God, what time have You selected
To free me from the cruel tyranny
That binds me without mercy to myself?

Chosen child—
In My Son
You are even now
Completely free.
Accept your freedom!
Walk out this very moment
Into the radiant company
Of My people.

I Can't—You Can

O, dear God—
It comes to me
With sweet and gentle relief
That this thing in my life
Which I can't possibly handle
Is the one thing above all
That You *can* handle.
You can handle it totally
And You can handle it now.

"Yes, dear child—
Now let Me!"

PERSONAL MESSAGE

Lord of my longing heart—
One early morning
As I struggled with desperate fear
You said softly but clearly
"Trust Me—you won't be disappointed."
That word has been with me ever since
And I am not disappointed.

VALENTINE'S DAY

This morning I opened Your Book
And read these magnificent words:
"See how very much
Our Heavenly Father loves us
For He allows us
To be called His children—
Think of it—and we really *are!*"
Then I remembered:
Today is February the fourteenth
Valentine's Day!
What a beautiful love message
From Your heart to mine:
I belong to You.
I really do!

THE TIME IS NOW

Lord
I see with startling clarity
That life is never long enough
To put You off
Until tomorrow.
The things that are before
Are all too soon behind.
I can never pick up
The years I've put down.
If I intend
To walk with You tomorrow
I must start today.

CHAPTER THREE

Family Treasures

BIRTHDAY DINNER

Here we are—just the two of us
Sitting across the table from each other
In this quaint old restaurant
With its nostalgic charm.
O Lord—
When my husband called to say
He had planned a birthday celebration
I had no idea we'd be coming here.

How pleasant it is, how peaceful
To relax without feeling pressured
To chatter aimlessly, happily
To laugh at our own foolish jokes . . .

As we wait for our entree
In the flickering candleglow
My thoughts are ribboned with tenderness.
How is it possible, dear Lord
How is it possible
That we should still feel
This dear mysterious newness
After so many years of marriage?
But that's the way it is with You:
The best is always just beginning.

FINAL DECISION

In this agonizing crisis, Lord
When my husband is jolted
By the twisted turn of events
And everything seems to be wrong
I desperately long to help him.
I ache to break the intense pressure—
To lessen the hurt and confusion.
Yet all I can do is listen.
I can be a sounding board
While he bounces back
Frustrations, fears, feelings.
I can be at his side
When he comes home depleted.
I can pray what I can't possibly say
For deep within me
I know the final decision
Has to be his.

Lord, that's not true:
The final decision
Has to be Yours.

MY DAD AND I

Dear Lord—
Today he's a stooped and withered old man
Slowly dragging himself along.
I can scarcely understand
His quavering words
As we walk in the chilling air.
The thought of crossing the street
Unnerves him completely.
He looks at me anxiously
With plaintive pleading in his eyes.

Lord, thirty years ago this very day
He stood strong and tall—
A distinguished educator
Addressing a class of collegians.
Vividly I remember
The thunderous applause
The rising ovation.
Proudly I watched
As students crowded upon him
Eager to clasp his hand.
Then together we strode

Over the rambling campus—
My arm linked through his.

Today, dear Lord
The scene is reversed:
As I carefully guide his shuffling steps
His arm is linked through *mine*.
We cross in front of the halting traffic
And I hear his whispered *thank-you*.
My heart throbs with poignant memories
With love
With deep gratitude
As we walk together—
My dad and I.

Lord, every path I've walked with Dad
Has led to You.

Lord, how deeply I cherish
My mother's Bible
With its worn leather cover—
Its frayed edges.
Slowly I turn the thin pages
And memories glisten
Between chapters and verses.
On every page, dear Lord
There are heart-prints of her:
Verses carefully underlined
Words neatly circled
Tiny arrows pointing to references
Secret desires written in margins.
How she loved Your Word, dear God.

I turn once more to the verse
She repeatedly quoted:
"And we know that all things
Work together for good
To them that love God . . ."
(Lord, the verse is tear-stained.
Her tears or mine?)
Gently now I touch the words
At the top of the page—

Written so laboriously
Five days before she left us:
Greater than the pain
That pulls me down
Is the power that pulls me up.

Dear God
Thank You for the Book of all books
And for quiet moments of reminiscing.
Just now Your love mingles with hers
And I am comforted.
I am sustained.

I Somehow Always Know

Lord—
I love to watch my husband
As he sits before an open hearth—
His eyes following the rhythmic flames
As they circle the massive logs.
Always his index finger
Is pressed against his cheek
And when I interrupt his thoughts
With just a word or two
I somehow always know
I've caught him
In the middle of a prayer.

My Children, My Children

O Lord
My children
My children!
I pray for them so earnestly
So achingly
So imploringly.
Day after day
Year after year
I continue to plead
I continue to intercede.
Are You listening, Lord?
Do You hear me?

Dear child
Not only do I hear you:
I'm interceding for them, too.

SACRED TRUST

Here she comes running
My five-year-old pixie:
Beautiful, delicate Pamela Sue.
Her eyes are full of laughter
Her voice is full of song
And on her soft pink lips
I detect the beginning of a kiss.
O, dear God—
Never can I thank You sufficiently
For entrusting this treasure—*to me.*

EARTH-BOUND

Tonight
My heart is hushed with quiet
Through and through.
A gentle stillness permeates our house.
I rest contentedly by my husband's side
As though I hadn't a care in the world.

Except . . .

I *know* I'll hear
That loud earth-jarring truck
At six o'clock in the morning
When the men pick up trash
On our street.

Lord, I'm so earth-bound.

OTHER HUSBANDS

So—other husbands
Come home late for dinner, too.
They rumple the paper
And leave shoes under the bed
And clutter the bathroom.
Other husbands gripe about budgets
And forget about birthdays
And steal the punch line
When you're telling a story.
Other husbands sulk like small boys
And refuse to admit they're wrong.
I made this amazing discovery today
While I lunched with four wives.
So no husband is perfect.
But thank You, dear Lord
That mine probably comes closest.

OBVIOUS ANSWER

In Your expansive economy, Lord
Love invariably includes responsibility.
This weight my husband shoulders
With solid integrity
And gentle fortitude.
Again today
He revealed his consistency
When he earnestly prayed:
"Make me everything a husband should be—
First for Your sake
And then for hers."

CHAPTER FOUR

Joy Follows Pain

MORE JOY IN SORROW

O God
When at last I was able
To say Yes to You
In the aching depth
Of my crushing loss—
Suddenly I found
More joy in sorrow
Than in all my previous joy.

NEVER ALONE

Lord God . . .
As I sit here silently
With my friend of many years
Please let her know how deeply I care.
How achingly I long to comfort
Her grief-stupored heart.
Make me just now a gentle transmitter
Of Your calming peace.
Her anguish is too deep for words—
At least my words, Lord.
She needs the solace of *Your* words
Whispered assuringly to her waiting heart.
In her new-born pain
You alone can sustain her.
In the long, tedious climb from rock-bottom
You alone can stabilize her.

Without You there is only despair
But praise upon praise
She is never without You!

I LISTEN . . .

God, without You
I am like a blind man
Groping to find my way
In the darkness.
Voices are calling from this place
And voices are calling from that place
But I am confused
I don't know where to turn.

Always I listen for Your voice
For You alone bring light
To my desolate being.

Still I brood and grope
In the darkness
As voices calling from this place
And voices calling from that place
Make the absence of Your voice
Ever more painful.

"And I will give thee the treasures of
darkness . . . "

(Isaiah 45: 3)

So Lonely

She is the victim of loneliness
Agonizing and acute.
She insists that her aloofness
Is a shield of protection
But around her empty heart
She wears an invisible sign:
"Please pay attention to me."
Her body is tense
And her voice is brittle
But her longings are fragile
And velvet-soft.
"Please pray for me,"
She often requests.
"I'm so tired of living alone
And plunging into depression.
I'm tired of explaining myself
And huddling in crowds like a sheep."

Lord, I do pray for her—
Earnestly, compassionately.
(Loneliness is a dreadful thing.)
You have given her consuming needs
Which beg for satisfaction.
May she offer herself as a gift to You
And open herself to receive from You . . .

And, Lord, while I pray for her
I pray with equal compassion
For desperate, lonely wives
Who never see the distant eyes
Hiding behind the newspaper.

ALL WILL BE WELL

O Lord God—
In the midst of consuming sorrow
When despair and loneliness hedge me in
You understand my frailties—
My hesitancies, my fears.
As I scamper from doubt to doubt
You forgive so quickly my outbursts.
Never do You drive me away
When I rail against You
In peevish rebellion.
When I scream
"Don't You even care?"
You quiet my fragmented heart.
You work in me silently
Always planning in love.
You refine me in the white-flamed
Furnace of uffliction.
In the silent darkness You whisper:
"Trust Me—all will be well."

Another marriage is shattered, Lord,
The divorce will be final next week.

He said it was the breakdown of communication
And the subtle infiltration of boredom.
She said it was an accumulation of things.
He said she was unnecessarily preoccupied
With home and children and activities.
She said he stifled her dreams
And ignored her achievements.
He said he felt imprisoned, restricted—
That night after night he got the old push-away.
She said he was harsh and brutal
And he often embarrassed her in public.
He said her critical attitudes
Contributed to his sense of inadequacy.
She said she felt lonely and unappreciated
With no claim to personal identity.
He said she wallowed in self-pity
And refused to acknowledge her benefits.
She said he was thriftless and irresponsible.
He said she didn't understand.
She said he didn't care.

Lord, how tragic.
Through all the wearisome years
Neither of them asked what *You* said.

SACRED ASSIGNMENT

Lord—
Here in my narrow hospital bed
I wait with brooding apprehension.
I trusted You exclusively
I prayed with fervent supplication.
I had so achingly hoped
You would touch and heal me
Without medication
Without the aid of man.
Wouldn't this give You great glory?
Wouldn't this enhance Your reputation?
I'm perplexed, Lord
I'm entangled in brambles of doubt
Surely You can extricate me . . . .

Dear child, listen!
I have a plan for your doctor, too.
I have given him the sacred assignment
Of becoming my instrument of healing
As we work together in your behalf.
So trust Me to create a double joy:
Yours and his.

CHANGE OF HEART

One night
In black and bitter agony
I cried, "No, Lord!
No! No!"
Then suddenly
I saw Your Cross.
I saw You enduring
Intolerable pain.
I saw the nails
The thorns
The drops of blood.
I saw Love
Nailed willingly to a tree.
Slowly, slowly
My turmoil melted
Until at last
My throbbing heart sobbed
"Yes, Lord!
Yes! Yes!"

RIGHTEOUS INDIGNATION

She began her explosive tirade
Over a cup of coffee.
(She insisted on calling it
Righteous indignation.)
"I'm tired of writing letters
To people who never answer.
I'm sick of sending birthday cards
And happy bits of cheer
Without any acknowledgments.
I'm *still* waiting
For a thank-you note
For an expensive wedding gift
I sent over a year ago."

I cautiously asked:
"Do you write to your family?"
"My family!" she mocked.
"At our last family reunion
We all agreed to write often.
So what happens?
I write regularly every month
Not ever knowing
If my letters are read.
I'm going to stop this
One-way correspondence.
I'll pray rather than write.
At least God will answer me."

Lord, maybe she's got a point.

MOVING AGAIN

Lord—
I feel desperately sorry for her.
So distressed, so disturbed.
Her family is moving again
(The fourth time in six years)
This time to a congested metropolis.
Her cry of revolt jolted me:
"I hate new schools.
Nobody talks to me.
The girls stare at me
And the boys snicker.
The worst part is—
I never have a best friend
And everybody needs a best friend."

O Lord—
In every cramped and crowded city
There are hundreds of children
Frightened and friendless
Lonely and longing.
Console my bewildered young friend

In her strange new environment.
Hold her close to Your tender heart
And be her very best Friend.

Then enable her to reach out
With a jump rope
With a lollipop
With smiling love
To other little girls
Who long so intensely
For one special friend.

UNFORGIVENESS

Dear Lord—
I thought of Faye again today
As I watched two little girls
Walk to school arm-in-arm . . .

Ours was a friendship of utter devotion:
We traded prizes from Cracker-Jacks
We shared hair clips and diary secrets
We whispered and giggled and wrote notes
Loyalty was our password.
But one day the lanky boy in my life
Discovered my friend was the prettier
And our friendship was sadly disrupted.
Lord, I can still recapture the hurt.
I was miserable and mean.
Words were harsh and unkind.
She begged for forgiveness
But I stubbornly refused:
"Wait until after vacation—
I might forgive you then . . . . "
But before our vacation had ended
My friend and her family had moved—
Leaving no forwarding address.
Lord, even now I wish I could tell her
Of the remorse I still feel
And the wound in my life
Because I refused to forgive.
Wherever she is, does she know?
I thought of her again today . . . .

HELP THEM JUST NOW

I keep thinking of them, Lord—
Thinking and thinking . . .

Sitting in the booth next to theirs
I heard but fragments
Of their troubled conversation.
She reproached him
For his thoughtlessness
His shameful unconcern.
With hatred in his voice
He whirled his bitter accusations—
Then he grabbed the check
And left her sitting there alone.
I wonder—is she still alone
This cold and rainy night?

Forgive me, Lord,
Please forgive me . . .

Too often I take for granted
The days
The nights
The gentle moments in-between
When my husband holds me close
And softly whispers:
"God was good to give me you."

YOURS IS THE GLORY

O Lord
This crushing problem I now face
Is so ludicrously impossible
To anyone but You—
How pleased You must be
With Your own secret solution
Which will give You all the glory.

YOU KNOW

O God
So many sleepless questions
Come trudging through the night
Round and round
Again and again . . .

Why did I decide so hastily?
What if I had waited?
Was my choice right?
How soon will I know?

And all the while, God
You know.

CHAPTER FIVE

A Little Child

I Don't Hear the Music

It was a difficult sheet of music.
Laboriously she struggled—
Measure by measure
Note by note.
Finally with ten-year-old exasperation
She pressed her fists into her cheeks:
"I *know* I'm playing the right notes
But I just don't hear the music."

O God, what a vivid portrait
Of our harassed and hectic lives:
We live in the right houses
Give to the right charities
And read the right books . . .
We sit in the right church pews
Speak to the right people
And smile the right smiles . . .
We buy the right clothes
And drive the right cars
And join the right clubs . . .
Yet, far too often
There's a mysterious emptiness—
A futility in the midst of activity.

The music is missing.
O God—
You alone can create new songs
In the depths of our jangled hearts.
Take over.
Rewrite our compositions
With melodies vibrant and clear.
May they be singable melodies
Rich and beautiful melodies—
Even in the midst of crashing crescendos.

THE NAME

Dear Lord
What a tribute You've paid
To the couple next door:
You've abundantly blessed them
With a strong healthy baby boy!
Finally they've agreed on his name.
I smiled when I saw
The long list of choices.
Everybody, it seems
From grandparents to cousins
Added their choice to the list.
I was thinking today, God,
There was never a choice
Nor was there ever a question
About the name of Your Son.
Before the foundation of the world
The fact was determined:
"And thou shalt call his name JESUS
For he shall save his people
From their sins."
JESUS—the Name above every name!

SUBTLE REMINDER

O Lord, thank You!
I love the way You teach me.

Remember how it happened?
I was quietly reading from Timothy:
"But godliness with contentment
Is great gain."
Then in the middle of lamenting
My own personal battle
With discontent
Jimmy came bursting in.
Churning with excitement
He insisted on showing me
The newest addition
To his menagerie of bugs:
"A beetle that's a boy!"

I managed sufficient enthusiasm
To welcome the new family friend
Before going back to Timothy.
Then I read it again—
The verse on contentment.
Suddenly, Lord, I chuckled aloud
At Your subtle reminder:

Often it's easier to find
"A beetle that's a boy"
Than a Christian who's content.

LONGER THAN TOMORROW

"Look, Mom—
I have to learn
This long list
By heart.
I've got to know it
By tomorrow.
Will you help me?"

Lord
I too have a long list
To learn *by heart:*
Patience . . .
Contentment . . .
Trust . . .
On and on it goes.
Will You help me?

But Lord
I'll need longer
Than tomorrow.

NEAT ARRANGEMENT

He sat in our kitchen
Gulping freshly baked cookies—
Football helmet under his stool.
I asked, "How are your mom and dad?"
Quick response:
"Fine as ever."
Brief pause:
"They sure kiss and hug a lot."
Between bites:
"It's OK—we have fun together."
Eyes full of mischief:
"Husbands and wives are a neat arrangement."

Lord, thank You for Rick's parents.
Bless them for the love they demonstrate
For the atmosphere they create—
The goals they stretch toward.
Thank You for lovable Rick
With all his zest and enthusiasm.
Keep him steady and stable, Lord—
Honest and clean—
With his values held high.
Add maturity to his young conviction:
"Husbands and wives are a neat arrangement."
Someday Lord, he'll kneel at the altar
(Frightened but elated)
With his own glowing bride.
On that day may he openly acknowledge You
As the One who wisely did the arranging.

BOOK-LENGTH NOVEL

Lord, as I hold her in my arms
And kiss her tiny fingers
I wonder if anyone in all the world
Has ever been as happy as I am now!
She's like a tiny poem
Short but beautiful—
And several years from now
She'll be a story.
Lord, I'm trusting You
To write the plot.
Then at last she'll be
A book-length novel
Translated into many languages.
I am confident of this, Lord
For You are both
Author and Publisher.

MUSIC LESSONS

Thank You, God
For the dear, gentle children
Who sit at my piano each week—
Children with merry eyes
And trusting smiles
And silly giggles that never stop.

Thank You for Jeff
With a pocket full of treasures
And a face full of freckles.
Bless him for playing one piece accurately
And for his shining words that day:
"You've got to go for the miracles!"
(God, You said so too.)

Thank You for Laurie
A wisp of lovely song.
Bless her for her pensive reflections
Her jeweled sensitivity:
"I guess the whole wide world
Has an ache in its heart."
(God, that's why You sent Jesus.)

Thank You for David
Who always laughs at his own jokes.
Bless him for his candid honesty:
"I'll practice real hard
When you trade in your piano for drums."
(God, keep me in step with Your drum.)

Thank You for Karen
Crisp and colorful as autumn.
Bless her for her innocent wisdom:
"Today I prayed for a good lesson."
"Did you practice?"
"Of course!
Why pray if you don't practice?"
(God, forgive me for too often
Blaming You for my poor production.)

I humbly ask You now
To accept my *fortissimo* praise
For the countless beautiful times
Your small friends
Have played a Symphony of Joy
In the Concert Hall of my tuned-in heart.

CHAPTER SIX

Reasons to Sing

You Wait for Me

Lord
I am so prone to
Extravagant extremes:
I either foolishly
Justify my imperfections
Or I frantically bemoan them.
All the while You wait for me
To release them—to You.

SAME SONG

Lord, I'm through!
Finished!
I obeyed Your instructions
I spoke as You directed.
Now what comes of it
Is Your responsibility:
I won't give it another thought.
"May I count on that, child?"
"Why do You ask, Father?"
"Child, we've been through this before."

MISERABLE

Today
As I moved into
The shadowy realm
Of jealousy and fear
I quickly discovered
I had moved out
Of the radiant realm
Of fellowship with You.
And, Lord
I was so miserably lonely.

I MET AN AUTHOR

Lord, I'm so excited
Because I met an author—
A real, live author—
Who's written at least
Seven "how-to" books.
I purchased his latest book
And he autographed it for me.
When I finished the last chapter
I couldn't help but wonder:
Do all the "how-to" authors
Really know how to?
If so, dear Lord
There's a lot of perfection
Right here on earth!

PAID IN FULL

It seemed so strange
To call a taxi today—
The first time in years!
With routine boredom
The driver set the meter
And the minutes began clicking away.
I watched closely
Hoping we'd avoid the detours
And at least some of the red lights.
Somehow, that meter clicked
With such persistent rapidity.
When I finally reached my destination
And paid the fare
I was thankful all over again
That I'm seldom without a car.
Thankful too, dear God
That when I reach
My heavenly destination
Your welcome words will be:
Paid in full!

JOY

Joy!
My favorite word.
Circumstances may determine my happiness,
But, Lord, You determine my joy.
Joy is sweetly honest.
No wonder the minister said:
"You can't hide joy if you have it—
You can't fake it if you don't."
Who can manufacture it, Lord?
Joy is Your creation.
Who may have it?
Anyone who asks.
Thank You, Lord
For joy!

FOREVER WORTHY

Dear God
I have sinned
Against Heaven
And against You.
I am no longer worthy
To be called Your child.

Child, I know . . . I know . . .
But My Son
Is forever worthy
To be called Your Savior.

Obvious Change

Yesterday, Lord
While I shopped with my dear friend
We were distinctly aware
Of an obvious change.
As we lingered at various counters
Every clerk casually asked
"May I help you, ladies?"
We finally consoled ourselves
With a cup of hot tea
And wistfully reminisced.
It seems such a short time ago
That the clerks were asking
"May I help you, girls?"

NOT AS THEY SEEM

It would seem, Lord
When You have been our dwelling place
In all generations . . .
When You have guided us
Undergirded us
And enveloped us with love . . .
When You are Bread for the hungry
Rest for the weary
Strength for the powerless
And Joy unspeakable . . .
It would seem, Lord
That we would have more to offer
Than lust
Greed
Hatred
War . . .

But that's precisely why
You came to die:
In the hearts of men
Things are not as they seem.

Premium Price

Lord
You have promised
That when You have tried me
I shall come forth as gold.

Gold at *premium* price, Lord?

CANCELLED OUT

I keep thinking about the man
Who sat behind me in church today.
After every prayer
After the choir anthem
And at least a dozen times
During the sermon
He shouted a boisterous *Amen*.
Then after the service
He shouted at his wife
As they walked toward their car
And, Lord, that angry shout
Cancelled all his Amens.

DIRECT ANSWER

O Lord
I've battled and struggled
I've dragged through
Tortured guilt-ridden hours
I've wept before You
Until there are no more tears.
What more can I do?

Dear child,
You can begin to obey!

WHY?

I'm singing today
In the midst of adversity —
Singing without reason for song.
Lord, do You want to know why?
Simply because I'm staunchly convinced
That as I continue my songs in the night
You'll create a new reason for singing.

DENIAL

Lord, one day You said
To Your disciples:
"If anyone wants
To be a follower of Mine
Let him deny himself . . . "
Then again You said to Peter:
"Before the cock crows at dawn
You will deny Me three times."

Lord, You bestir me
With a demanding truth:
You've given me a choice
And the choice is always mine.
I must deny myself
Or I must deny You.

FLOW OF ADVICE

She's never been married
But she seems better informed
On how to handle a husband
Than any wife I know.
She's never had children
But her knowledge of child-raising
Is as expansive as the sky.
I really want to be her friend
But please help her, Lord
To be a little more charitable
And a little less verbal
With her free flow of advice.
I'd like to welcome her without wincing
When I see her come up the walk.

FREE!

I am tingling with the joy
Of a glorious discovery:
Continuous surrender
Brings continuous freedom.
Lord, I love being free!

PERSONAL HURT

O God—
In this personal hurt
That pierces so deeply
Give me, I pray
The high and holy privilege
Of proving to the one
Who initiated the hurt
That the love of Jesus
Can withstand it.

TRAGIC WASTE

How foolish
That I worry so, Lord.
(A tragic waste
Of Your Life in me.)
After all
I can't imagine
You sitting here
Worrying about tomorrow.

PROMOTION

Dear God:
I resign.

Dear child:
Good!
Now I'll promote you.

QUESTION AND ANSWER

"Oh, what a terrible
Predicament I'm in!
Who will free me from my slavery
To this deadly lower nature?"

Lord, Paul's question
Is my question
But I'm sick of forever
Repeating the question.
Push me on
To the glorious answer:
"Thank God!
It has been done
By Jesus Christ our Lord.
He has set me free."

DOTING PARENTS

Lord, correct me if I'm wrong
But it seems to me
Those doting parents down the street
Could express their love
More genuinely
And far more effectively
If they were a little less *doting*
And a little more *don'ting*.

SURPRISE

Whenever I begin to be certain
Of the way You're going to work—
When I insist You will use
This method
This plan
This instrument
Just as You did before—
I'm always caught completely off guard:
That's exactly the time
You choose a startling new way.

ONE SAD AND BITTER TIME

My Lord—
One sad and bitter time
My estranged heart said:
"No—I don't want Your will.
I want freedom to do my will."
You gave me my request
And sent leanness to my soul.
One sad and bitter time . . .

JUST CRY

Lord, the sky is black and ominous
And all sense of Your presence is gone.
I am utterly devoid of energy
I am thwarted at every turn
My fragmented thoughts
Refuse to form words
All I can bring to You
Is my anguished cry.

Then cry, dear child
Just cry.

CHAPTER SEVEN

He Promises Spring

AFTER

Lord
Since she whom we love
Is with You
We are like guests
Who wearily stayed at the table
To make small-talk
And sip lemonade
After the hostess had gone to bed.

THE KING IS COMING

I watched and smiled
As my silver-haired grandmother
Listened with rapt attention
To the intellectual speaker.
It was indeed a stimulating
Prophetic study
Of things to come.
On our way home I asked:
"Did you enjoy it?"
"Oh yes, my dear!
I didn't understand it all
But it doesn't matter:
I know the *One* who is coming."

MY RADIANT DAWN

Dear God—
The psalmist David said
He watched for You
As one who waits for the dawn.

I know, God—
I know . . .

One who waits for the dawn
Waits in quivering darkness
In loneliness
In somber silence . . .
He waits for that
Which comes slowly—
Ever so slowly . . .
But God—
He waits for that
Which He *knows* will come
And when it comes
At last there is light!

I am waiting
As David waited.
O God,
You *will* come—
My Radiant Dawn!

THE TRUST OF THE UNEXPLAINED

Lord of my aching heart:
He was so young
So very young
With all of life before him.
Exuberant, vital
Full of promise, of breathless wonder.
Gifted, intelligent, sensitive
Always inquisitive
Eager to learn, to know, to do.
A dreamer, a schemer
Eyes full of merriment
Heart full of laughter
Venture in his blood
Mischief in his fingers
Challenge in his thoughts
So many plans, so many hopes
Admired by his teachers
Extolled by his friends
Loved, so dearly loved . . .

Lord, no longer dare I beat my fists
Upon the walls of Heaven.
I am too weary, too sorrow-consumed.
I know now that ten thousand why's
Will never bring him back.
In pitch darkness I have shouted my why's.
My reward? A sea of shadowed silence.
What is left?
What more shall I ask?
Just this, dear God:
Think through me Your thoughts
Create within me Your peace
Until there is born in my aching heart
"The trust of the unexplained."

I PROMISE YOU SPRING

O God . . . God
On this sullen winter day
When the sky is threatening
And the driving wind
Pushes against our small house
I walk from room to room
Tortured, twisted, torn.
Without a whispered warning
Without a turn or a touch
You have taken my dearest love—
And I am left utterly defenseless
In the cruel, crushing arms
Of intolerable grief.
I am lost and listless
Waves of despair crash over me
I am bereft of love, of joy.

Do You understand, God?
There is no splendor anymore.
There is no magic, no laughter.
There is no one who speaks my language
Or reads my thoughts
Or gentles my turbulent heart.
O God—there are two winters now
And the winter within me

Is by far the most dismal.
Do You understand?

"Child of My love:
In My infinite Plan
There are four seasons.
Trust Me . . . Trust Me . . .
I promise you—*Spring.*"

While She Waits

Lord
They hadn't wanted it like this—
Nor had they anticipated
The sudden drastic change.
Faithfully, with infinite patience
He'd taken care of her
Day by day, year after year.
He'd fixed her meals
Helped her into her clothes—
Even combed her thinning hair.
He'd read to her by the hour
Written short notes
And fluffed the pillows
Behind her aching back.
Theirs was a beautiful devotion
And now he's gone
And she is so desperately lonely.
Today between choking sobs
She told me how she longed to join him.
Surely You understand, dear Lord.
Take her with You soon, I pray.
Give her her heart's desire.
And while she waits
May those of us who love her
Do what we can to make the lonely hours
A little less painful.

"HAVE A NICE FOREVER"

Even at longest, Lord
Life is fleetingly short—
A mere breath
A withering flower
A shadow in a pantomine.
It sobers me
That I am but a passing occupant
A temporary guest who says hello
Then so suddenly—good-bye.

But, Lord—
You have chosen me
To be Your very own.
The instant You call my name
I shall be a permanent resident
In my Father's house.
Once again
With ecstatic joy
I shall say hello—
But never through all Eternity
Shall I have to say good-bye!

SUDDENLY MINE

O Lord
May I believe in the darkness
When all hope has vanished
When waves beat with fury
And no star lights my sky.
May I believe without
Feeling or knowing or proving
Till one shining moment when
You shatter the darkness
And all I believed for
Is suddenly mine.

GOLDEN ANNIVERSARY

Just think, dear Lord—
Today they are celebrating
Their golden wedding anniversary!
She is like a youthful bride
Still flushed with dreams
And he smiles at her
As though it were their wedding day.
In the reception line I asked:
"Does it seem like fifty years?"
Her blue eyes glistened
As she grabbed my hand.
"My dear, we're still just kids.
Think what God has waiting for us
When we're both with Him."

CHAPTER EIGHT

Celebrating His World

AT LAST I KNOW

Today, dear God
I stood on the sunlit shore
And watched two laughing children
Try to put the whole wide sea
Into a shiny pail.
And now at last I know
Why I stammer so
When I try to put my rushing joy
Into a prayer.

MAJESTIC APPROVAL

O God—
I'd love to keep
The beauty of this day
Forever and forever:
The sky incredibly blue
New leaves shining
Flowers swaying
In the gentle breeze
Birds with changeful wills
Darting here and there
The lake a sparkling jewel
Surrounded by spicy pines
And You looking down
At Your handiwork
With majestic approval.

On Second Thought

Thank You, Lord—thank You so much
For a delicious sense of accomplishment
After pulling stubborn weeds
In the hot August sun.
Thank You for a tub of warm water
Fragrant with bath oil
Glistening with pink suds.
Thank You for a wide, colorful towel
Tossed carelessly by the side of the tub.
Thank You for a firm comb and brush—
For a nail-file and toothpaste
And smooth, creamy lotion.

Thank You for a fresh surge of energy
For renewed eagerness
And a joyful sense of well-being.
For some strange reason
I even feel pretty today!
Lord, I wouldn't say that to anyone else.
After all—
With bulges here and there
And wrinkles beginning to show
Who but my husband would call me pretty?

On second thought
Maybe You would, Lord.
Your Word comes flashing:
God hath made everything beautiful in His time . . .

Your time is always Now.
Thank You, Lord.

SCATTERED THOUGHTS

Dear God
As the luminous sky
Holds a million scattered stars
Please hold my scattered thoughts
And illumine them *with You*.

ENOUGH FAMILY

Really, Lord
He's a ridiculously
Homely little dog.
Look at him
With his drooping tail
And his crumpled ear.
Besides, if there's anything
We don't need around here
It's another dog.
But what could I do
Against an argument like this:
"*Mother!* How could you turn your back
On God's poor homeless creature?"
So, who's pouring warm milk
For God's poor homeless creature?
Me—the mother who vehemently declared:
"No more dogs!"
Lord, if he belongs to somebody
Please help us to find out soon.

After all—
One husband three children
Two dogs two cats
One parakeet four goldfish
And a pet lizard
That frightens me to death—
Isn't that enough family
For one mother to manage?

MOMENTS OF LEISURE

Lord, thank You
For the moments of leisure
And peaceful solitude
I can legitimately snatch
Here and there
Without apologizing.
Thank You for assuring me
That I needn't condemn myself
When I spend some time
Reading or resting
Or shopping just for fun.
Thank You for convincing me
That there's no glory
In a rat race.
I've discovered, dear Lord
That an hour or two
"Away from it all"
Calms my inner muddle
And cuts through the confusion.
Without a driving sense of urgency
I think more clearly—
I plan more wisely.
I am more patient, more loving
More understanding with my family.
I even accept with calmness
The multiple demands imposed upon me.

Thank You so much, dear God
For the certain knowledge that Jesus
(Who always obeyed the Father)
Went apart from the crowd to rest.
So must I!

NEW RECIPE

Thank You, Lord,
For this luscious new salad
I'm preparing for our dinner—
And for the kindness of the friend
Who shared the recipe.
Thank You for the joy of creativity
For the satisfaction of achievement.
Thank You for sufficient money
To buy the necessary ingredients
For the blue bowl I'm using
To mix and season
For the utensils to measure and stir.
Thank You for the eagerness to sample it
For the hunger to relish it
For the health to digest it.
Thank You for the anticipation of my family
And for their excitement over a new recipe.
Thank You for their expressive appreciation:
"Wow, Mom! This is way out."

Goodness, Lord
What a wealth of blessing
You've wrapped up
In one new salad.
Thank You!
Tonight at the dinner table
We'll remember to thank You again.

HAPPY NEW YEAR

This very first day
Of the fresh new year
I sing a new song—
A joyful, exalted song!
With Israel's sweet singer I exclaim:
"How good it is to sing God's praise
How delightful and how right."
The volume increases
The tempo accelerates
With glorious anticipation
I shout a rousing welcome
To the up-and-coming days.
The future cannot daunt me
Every inscrutable mystery
Becomes a consolation of joy
For with You in control, dear God
The worst may happen
But the best is yet to come.

AND FOR EVER

Lord, Your Word
Assuredly declares
You are the same

Yesterday . . .
Shimmering sunlight
Swelling song

And today . . .
Sudden storm
Sullen sighs

And for ever . . .
" . . . lo, I am with you alway,
even unto the end of the world."

I LOVE IT, LORD

What in the world
Is going on today, Lord?
Why the big celebration?
The fragrance of lilacs
The shimmering sound of birds
The red-gold sky
The air blue and sweet
The sudden burst of pink bloom
A thirsty vine
The shout of mountains miles around . . .
Really, Lord
What's happening?

Is it—
Could it be
That Spring has made her debut?
Is that why
You've dressed all of Nature
In party clothes?

Whatever the reason
I love it, Lord.
Thank You!

I SHOUT YES

Lord, this
Is the very first day
Of an unblemished new year.
For the year finally finished
I thank You.
To the year newly born
I shout—Yes!

MORE
rewarding reading...
from Cook

A

LIVING UNAFRAID. Do you have fears? Most people do—and this book tells about some who overcame their fears by applying an age-old truth: "Thou alone, O Lord, makest me to live unafraid." Read their stories . . . gain encouragement from their victories. By Dr. Charles W. Keysor, director of publications, Asbury College.   86439—$1.25

PEBBLES OF TRUTH. Poems for all Christians, on topics of basic interest: the love of God . . . faith . . . repentance . . . forgiveness . . . salvation . . . obedience . . . fellowship . . . freedom . . . rejoicing . . . loyalty. By Dr. William S. Stoddard, pastor of Walnut Creek (Calif.) Presbyterian Church. Illustrated.   86371—$1.25

THEIR FINEST HOUR. Engrossing biographies of people whose dedication to Christ still inspires those who share their faith. Some names you will recognize . . . others, not. For instance: William A. "Devil Anse" Hatfield. His conversion ended the most publicized feud in America's history! Photos. By Charles Ludwig.   82917—$1.95

THE PROPHET OF WHEAT STREET by James W. English. In hard cover, it was the choice of six book clubs! English, former editor of Boys' Life, tells the story of William Borders, a southern black Northwestern graduate who returned to lead Atlanta's black church to revitalized faith, improved housing, new self-respect.   72678—$1.25

ALCOHOLISM by Pastor Paul. Encouragement for alcoholics, and all who are concerned about them—a pastor tells how God helped him beat the bottle. Although well educated and respected, the author found release not through his own efforts alone, but through the help of God . . . and those who offered their strength.   72629—$1.95

O CHRISTIAN! O JEW! by Paul Carlson. A member of Christians Concerned for Israel, Pastor Paul Carlson traces the progress of prophecy . . . from God's covenant with Abraham to the miracle of modern-day Israel. He presents a seldom-seen side of Jewish-Christian relations to help Christians better understand Jews.   75820—$1.95

B

LET'S SUCCEED WITH OUR TEENAGERS by Jay Kesler. An eminent authority, the president of Youth for Christ International, offers a new understanding of the age-old but desperately new problems even the happiest of families must face: coming of age, discipline and love, peer pressure, drugs, alcohol, tobacco, the Church. 72660—$1.25

BEFORE I WAKE. Are you ready to face death—your own death, or the death of a loved one? Both philosophical and practical, this book by Pastor Paul R. Carlson presents the Christian view of the nature and destiny of man, draws on doctors, psychologists, lawyers and morticians to help one face grief, make a will, arrange a funeral. 86454—$1.50

CHRISTIANS IN THE SHADOW OF THE KREMLIN by Anita and Peter Deyneka, Jr. Why can't the rulers of Russia banish faith? They've closed churches, taught atheism in the schools —yet a vital (if unorganized) church remains. How can it be? Come and learn as the authors talk with Russian students, workers, professional people. Photos. 82982—$1.50

THE EVIDENCE THAT CONVICTED AIDA SKRIPNIKOVA by Michael Bourdeaux. This book places its reader at the side of a young Russian girl on trial. She chooses imprisonment to the abandonment of faith in a story that challenges ALL Christians. (Bourdeaux is a worker at London's Center for Study of Religion and Communism.) 72652—$1.25

HOW SILENTLY, HOW SILENTLY. Joseph Bayly's modern-day fables and fantasies lead to spiritual discoveries: The wise computer's treatise on whether or not Man exists. The boy who arrives at college with shields of pure gold and returns home with shining shields that nobody recognizes as brass. The Israeli, in America at Christmas—who was he? 73304—$1.25

LOOK AT ME, PLEASE LOOK AT ME by Clark, Dahl, and Gonzenbach. Two church women tell about their work with the mentally retarded, how concern led them through fear and revulsion to acceptance and love—also to the discovery that often behind the facade of physical unloveliness waits a warm and responsive personality. 72595—$1.25

C

FAITH AT THE TOP by Wes Pippert. The author, a seasoned UPI reporter in Washington, D.C., takes us into the lives of 10 prominent men and women who dared to bring Christ along with them on their way to the top—like Sen. Mark Hatfield, pro football star Charley Harraway, former NBC-TV reporter Nina Herrmann.   75796—$1.50

INVISIBLE HALOS by David C. Cook III. As the largest publisher of non-denominational Sunday School materials reaches the 100-year mark, its president and editor-in-chief presents this inspiring series of vignettes: unlikely heroes, people he has met during his busy life who have served for him as models of Christianity in action.   77289—$1.50

WHAT ABOUT HOROSCOPES? by Joseph Bayly. Is there reality behind them? Can they really foretell the future? In giving the answers to these questions, the author examines not only astrology, but mediums (and the "spirit world"), Satanism, witches, possession by demons, ESP—the whole range of "in" occult topics.   51490—95¢

WHAT A WAY TO GO! by Bob Laurent. For adults . . . to pass along to young people! They'll like singer-evangelist Laurent's conversational style and understanding approach. Bringing new faith to thousands, he packs solid Christian advice under catchy labels like Saved, Satisfied, and Petrified . . . and Jesus Signed My Pardon.   72728—$1.25

CAMP DEVOTIONS by Dick and Yvonne Messner. Like Jesus, Christians can use the glories of nature as inspiring object lessons—on a mountain, during a sunrise, near a lake. Each short, one-subject devotional offers site suggestion, Scripture text, theme, and prayer. (Yvonne Messner is a camp founder and teacher of camping.)   75945—$1.95

CAMPFIRE COOKING by Yvonne Messner. Pack-along guidebook to fixing tasty, nutritious meals from scratch in the out-of-doors. What utensils are needed? What preparation and cooking methods should be used? Which recipes are best? How can a group get the most from its time and money? A camper tells you. Illustrated   75937—$1.95

D